Th

Pocket Book of Tarot

Edited and Introduced

by

Jack Barrow

Published by
Winged Feet Productions, England
Esoteric Publishing

Published by Winged Feet Productions,
Hemel Hempstead, England.

A catalogue record for this book is available from the British Library

ISBN: 978-0-9515329-4-2
BIC subject category: VXC/VXW
Cover production by Rycraft Associates,
Trowbridge, England
Printed by CPI Antony Rowe, Eastbourne
on recyclable, biodegradable paper
taken from sustainable sources

Jack Barrow is the author of

The Hidden Masters
and the Unspeakable Evil

and also

Satanic Viruses:
The fall of the Roman Empire and how to bring it about

He is drawn to the occult and has been a student of the mysteries for many years

Dispatches

Thanks go to the original members of
The Alembic, without whom, not only would
these definitions not have been distilled,
but almost everything since
might not have taken place

Special thanks also for the use of
The Sheridan Douglas Tarot
ISBN 978-0-9553738-0-0
www.sheridandouglas.co.uk
Sheridan Douglas Press
12a Cinque Ports Street
Rye, East Sussex
TN31 7AD

For Feg

… and his good mate Dave,
whom I met only once

The Hidden Masters'

Pocket Book of Tarot

Contents

Introduction

The Three Hidden Masters, two from Hemel Hempstead and one from Bricket Wood are a group of magicians—not stage magicians mind you—for they are ritual magicians, and they are legendary, if you are in the know. They are in the habit of becoming involved in adventures, saving the Universe and all that, mostly at the weekends. For the truth of the matter is, if there can ever be such a thing as truth, that they have to be back at work on Monday mornings. Amongst their number is Nigel, famed for his oracular eye and his insight with the Tarot cards, astrology or other systems of divination.

Back in the old days—before magick became fashionable and the thought of putting pagan on your census form was just a silly idea—Nigel was involved in a magickal group with a fellow Hidden Master and one time mentor, Geoff who now lives in Blackpool. Geoff is no longer Nigel's mentor as all students at some point move on from their guru. However, there was a time when Nigel and Geoff worked together, attempting to unravel the mysteries of the Universe while drinking too much dark rum and developing other habits that they would one day use magick to overcome.

During that period the afore mentioned magickal group decided to tackle the Tarot to establish a consensus for use in ritual, path-working or other collective activities. What followed was a period of intense study, introspection and frequent bouts of drunkenness with occasional flashes of divine inspiration. Why else would one indulge in bouts of drunkenness other than in a search for enlightenment?

They spent some time studying the teachings of many of the major luminaries of the occult, including Hermes Trismegistus, Dr. John Dee,

Eliphas Levi, Jim Beam, McGregor Mathers, Lemuel Johnstone, Aleister Crowley, J. R. “Bob” Dobbs, A. E. Waite, Gerald Gardner and others. The conclusion that they came to was that some of them were quite probably drunk, mad or even fictitious, but they thought the same might be said of themselves so who were they do judge?

However, they did manage to distil a selection of definitions of the Tarot that condensed the teachings of these scholars of the mysteries. It is these definitions that are revealed in this book.

The Tarot

Back in the early eighties, when Nigel, Geoff and their magickal friends developed these definitions, Nigel used to carry a set of notes on the Tarot. Because his oracular powers were still in development he would frequently draw upon them as he learned to ply his trade. You are encouraged to do the same. Carry this book with you as you practice on your friends and don't be shy to look up references as you need to. Over time you will notice that you need them less and less. As Geoff once told Nigel, "Keep these definitions hidden handily under the table and you will never be stuck for a line in mystical bullshit!"

The Tarot can be used to portray much that can be experienced in human existence. The pages that follow describe, in the briefest terms possible, some key words for each card.

As the diligent and assiduous student of the occult that you undoubtedly are (why else would you have bought this book?) you will notice that the same word sometimes appears in relation to more than one card. This is because each card is describing an experience in the context of its suit. The four suits describe matters in relation to:

- Energy of many types (*Fire/Rods*)
- Emotion in all its forms (*Water/Cups*)
- The mind including all its strengths and weaknesses (*Air/Swords*)
- Material matters and how we manage them (*Earth/Pentacles*)

Therefore, the *Six of Rods* is described as 'success,' where it represents success as the culmination of a period of endeavour through work and effort. On the other hand the *Nine of Pentacles* is described as 'success' but in material terms which give security and comfort through wealth. The Rods card is concerned with motivation and effort while the Pentacles card is concerned with more mundane or material matters.

Interestingly, the occurrence of the Pentacles card might well be the outcome of living through the Rods card at an earlier stage in life, but that should come as no surprise for recognising connections between cards is a substantial part of the essence of the Tarot.

In the same way that the cards do not exist in isolation to each other, each of the suits does not exist in isolation either and they can even be seen as a series of stories that run together. Very few human experiences can be represented by a single element with subtle flavours and blends of other aspects visible at all times. Often this is a consequence of the nature of our language, but it is also an indication of the interconnectedness of all things. However, let's not get into all that interconnectedness stuff right now.

The suits can be seen as four stories—the story within the Major Arcana is more difficult to see—and the full deck has its own message.

So, there will be times when the viewer will see the footprints (and more) of other elements where they might not be expected. This doesn't change the nature of these elements—the heart is still concerned with matters of Water and the foundation of the world will always be the Earth—but the heart can always care about matters of the Earth; for have you never cared deeply for the place where you make your home?

Throughout the definitions you will also see two sets of key words, the second set described as the 'reversal'.

Much of the symbolism stems from Hermeticism where a comprehensive set of correspondences began to develop. Some scholars, such as Crowley, suggest that if the full set of Hermetic symbolism is represented in the upright interpretations of the cards then there is no need for such reversals. However, other students of the Tarot have been using reversals for many years, and it is for this reason that Nigel and his friends included them all those years ago. You can decide to use reversals or not depending on preference.

Rods

The suit of Rods or Wands or Staves represents the element of Fire.

Fire, in the Tarot, is related to things concerning energy. Energy can manifest in many ways from the physical energy of hard work to energy in terms of drive, enthusiasm or motivation. It is the energy of making things happen, either physically or mentally. It is about effort or sheer bloody minded will power.

The symbol of the Rod is simple to understand for it is a simple thing. The Rod is a blunt instrument. After all the Staff, or a simple stick, is perhaps the most basic of weapons. To understand this think of that scene at the beginning of *2001: A Space Odyssey* where the ape picks up a bone (a stick) and soon the ape's group are defeating the larger ape tribe. This is an act of will with the simplest of blunt instruments, the Rod.

However, the Rod need not be considered a purely offensive weapon. Indeed, it can be used to impose one's will on another, but it can also be used defensively, held up as a barrier in-front of oneself saying 'none shall pass.'

An important point to make is that the Rod should be stout. Among the fluffy bunny element of the pagan movement there can sometimes be a tendency for a *wand* to be seen as a finely crafted delicate thing with gem stones and fragile decorations all about. This might fit well with the teen witch movement that appreciates the paganism portrayed on the TV or in children's books but this is *not* the Rod of the Tarot. If the wand is not solid enough to be used as a club then the symbolism is wrong and the Tarot is all about symbolism.

In the days of the last millennium, when Nigel and Geoff were researching Tarot definitions, they also made new magical weapons and the Rod was the first thing they made. Deciding they needed a consecration with a bit of oomph, they consecrated them in physical combat. One sunny Saturday afternoon, at a local abandoned quarry, they used their new Rods as weapons against each other and, in turn, defended themselves with the same. They came away with Rods that carried the scars of the battle (each bore some of the wood stain or paint from the opponent Rod) and for a week or two their hands and forearms bore scrapes and bruises from the joust. Most importantly, each magician came away with a deeper understanding of what the Rod represents. A crystal encrusted wand from the local hippie shop simply wouldn't have survived.

Furthermore, the Rod is more than a weapon for acts of will relative to other people. Perhaps it's most important use is for the magician acting upon the self.

There is no such thing as a lazy magician for motivation is all. To become a magician requires discipline and a large part of this discipline is related to the will.

Acts of will within the individual can take many forms: the wilful decision to act; followed by the conscious act of planning; and the controlled implementtation of that plan; advantage can then be gained from a disciplined approach; with determination to win through against opposition; with success resulting from one's own determination; gaining willpower to stand firm against adversity; with resolution for commitment; and the considered application of resources; and finally the sheer bloody minded determination to shoulder a burden when it simply has to be done. That is the suit of Rods.

Rods = Fire = Will

Ace of Rods

Energy; opportunity; new beginnings; new growth

Reversal:

Tyranny; lassitude; decadence; missed opportunity; still born ideas and projects

Two of Rods

Will used with judgement; dominion; responsibility

Reversal:

Weakness; melancholy

Three of Rods

New enterprises or projects; commerce

Reversal:

Toil; disappointment; still born ventures

Four of Rods

Firm base; foundation for ideas; success; harvest home

Reversal:

Insecure base; undermining influences

Five of Rods

Competition; confidence; action; hustle; determination to win through

Reversal:

Lack of confidence; giving up at the first hurdle

Six of Rods

Success; victory in endeavour

Reversal:

Treachery; failure due to over confidence

Seven of Rods

Standing firm against adversity; the immovable object

Reversal:

Indecision; falling back under pressure

Eight of Rods

Willpower in motion; swiftness; commitment

Reversal:

False starts; indecision

Nine of Rods

Good arrangement of resources; perseverance; consolidation

Reversal:

Bad planning; blindness to realities

Ten of Rods

Burden of ambition; responsibilities; karma

Reversal:

Giving up; irresponsibility

Page of Rods

A messenger; new ideas; a different approach

Reversal:

Bad ideas; impractical schemes

Knight of Rods

New horizons or directions; travel, usually for the better

Reversal:

As above but usually for the worse

Queen of Rods

A dark woman, forceful, matriarchal

Reversal:

The same but vengeful and domineering

King of Rods

Honesty; integrity; willpower; force tempered by judgement; statesmanship

Reversal:

Corruption; tyranny; dictatorship

Cups

The suit of Cups or Chalices represents the element of Water.

Water, in the Tarot, is related to things concerning emotion. Emotion covers everything from relationships with others to the feelings within us that nobody can perceive apart from ourselves.

The symbol of the Cup is a container for our emotions, for were we not to control them they would control us. Water would run through our fingers, out of control, unless we contain it.

Emotions are a paradox for they are often the reason for living. Without feelings, from simple pleasures right through to the love of another person, our lives would be empty. However, if we were governed by our emotions we might not survive in a world full of millions of other individuals.

As we grow we learn to understand our feelings and not be ruled by them. A small child will burst into tears at the slightest stress or throw a tantrum if its will is thwarted, but we soon learn not to be ruled by these feelings. This process is called maturation.

This then, is the paradox of emotion. Without emotion our lives would be empty, but if they are allowed to rule us completely emotions would ruin our lives and possibly those of others. So a life without feeling would be cold and empty of joy and passion. Conversely, unbridled desire might result in self indulgence. Unhappiness allowed to take over our lives might result in despair. Anger at another person, if not managed, might result in violence or even murder. Uncontrolled lust might end in assault or rape.

The Cup is a subtle instrument to allow us to manage the subtle nature of our many feelings. Emotional development begins within us perhaps with the simplest of feelings such as sheer joy; we soon realise that others are important to us from simple friendship to full blown love; these relationships bring us fulfilment; but endless joy can soon become meaningless; as we mature we learn that we can even benefit from negative experiences; and discover that as life moves on we take positive experiences with us; but we must be mindful of our desires lest we lose touch with reality; for sometimes the only way is to take control of our emotions and withdraw; as contentment and smugness are easily confused; and we eventually realize that true fulfilment lies in simple relationships and inner joy. That is the suit of Cups.

Cups = Water = Emotion

Ace of Cups

Joy; contentment; fertility
Reversal:
Despair; emotional instability; treachery

Two of Cups

Friendship; love; union; sympathy
Reversal:
Jealousy; parting; temporary separation; false love

Three of Cups

Pleasure; fulfilment; plenty
Reversal:
Self indulgence; superfluity; disillusionment

Four of Cups

Discontent (and bored) with present conditions; longing for change; weariness; ennui

Reversal:

New instruction; new relationships; moving on

Five of Cups

Some loss in the process of receiving something such as a disappointing inheritance; loss but with something remaining

Reversal:

A new path; more gain than loss

Six of Cups

Nostalgia; memories

Reversal:

Possibility of clinging too much to the past; being stuck in the past

Seven of Cups

Imaginations stronger than reality; unreality; visions; illusory success; grasshopper mind

Reversal:

Resolution; design; decision; determination

Eight of Cups

A withdrawal from the present situation; retreat from emotional entanglement

Reversal:

Emotional entanglement; self sacrifice

Nine of Cups

Smug contentment; feelings of success; wish fulfilled; material happiness

Reversal:

Mistakes; imperfections; wish unfulfilled; vanity

Ten of Cups

Contentment; home life; fulfilment; security; trust

Reversal:

Loss of harmony; disturbance is due; debauchery; decadence

Page of Cups

A fair young man or woman; a studious and artistic youth; growing up

Reversal:

Deception; obstacles of all kinds; emotionally immature; selfish

Knight of Cups

Arrival; a silver tongued devil

Reversal:

Fraud; cunning; abuse of confidence; confidence trickster

Queen of Cups

A good fair woman, honest and devoted, loving; intelligence; success; happiness; imagination; intuition; pleasure; wisdom

Reversal:

A woman not to be trusted; vice; dishonour; perverse; a woman scorned

King of Cups

A fair man; creative intelligence; a man of compassion; business; art

Reversal:

Dishonest; double dealings; scandal; injustice; considerable loss

Swords

The suit of Swords represents the element of Air.

Air, in the Tarot, is related to things concerning the mind. In the Tarot the mind covers everything from reason and logic, analysis and intellect, as well as communication.

The symbol of the Sword is quite specific in that it is usually depicted as a double edged weapon, quite plain and unadorned. These details are quite important as they relate specifically to the meaning of the Sword.

It is double edged because the mind can work in your favour or against you. Analysis is usually a good thing, but in some circumstances, such as when there is a lack information, it can lead to indecision, confusion or even a loss of touch with reality.

Being depicted as plain the Sword can be likened to Occam's razor. A little research will yield more detail but, suffice to say, the idea of Occam's razor says that *when it comes to matters of intellect the simplest ideas are often the best*. If the Sword were covered in decorations, be they gems and jewels, engravings or sigils, they would lend the Sword to being beautiful. Beauty is an aspect of the Cup for beauty is in the eye of the emotional beholder. The lack of adornment as usually depicted on Swords in the Tarot represents objectivity or detachment. To be objective is to be uninfluenced by considerations of emotion, practicality or any other factor that might influence our intellectual understanding of any matter. The Sword is a functional weapon as should be the magician's intellect.

Of course the idea of Occam's razor is an ideal and very few of us are ever truly objective. Ultimately it is impossible to be completely detached as each of us is a bundle of motivations, desires, ideas and practical considerations. From these influences we try to extract an understanding of anything we consider.

So examining the Swords suit, where you might expect to see objectivity, the interpretations are peppered with references to things that you might expect to find in the other suits. That is the paradox of the human relationship with the mind.

Acts of intellect begin with inspiration, perhaps coming from the previous suit; but very soon decisions need to be made; however indecision can lead to delay; and too much introspection can lead to isolation; which can result in loss or worse; sometimes the only solution is to move on; and to plan future strategies; sometimes the only option is to seek advice; for dwelling on matters without the right information can lead to despair; which can only end in tears. That is the suit of Swords.

Swords = Air = Reason

Ace of Swords

Starting point; inspiration; triumph of force; conquest

Reversal:

Disaster; pain; conception

Two of Swords

Decision time; balanced force; meeting of minds

Reversal:

Ill-decisions; disloyalty; falsehood; duplicity

Three of Swords

Rupture; delay; sorrow

Reversal:

Error of judgement; loss; aversion

Four of Swords

Rest from strife; exile;
reluctance to face opposition
Reversal:
Change for the better;
beginnings of a plan; certain
success after wise administration

Five of Swords

Loss; humiliation; partial or
pyrrhic victory; defeat
Reversal:
Sorrow; mourning

Six of Swords

Journey (possibly) by water;
passage from difficulties;
resolution of difficulties through
another person
Reversal:
Dilemma without any immediate
solution

Seven of Swords

Wishes; hopes; attempts; a plan that will only work with strategy; annoyance to others

Reversal:

Instruction; good advice probably neglected

Eight of Swords

Crisis; slander; inability to get out of a difficult situation; help or information needed from others

Reversal:

Opposition; accident; treachery; fatality

Nine of Swords

Desolation; failure; despair; suffering generally

Reversal:

Shame; suspicion; imprisonment; a bad omen

Ten of Swords

Pain; tears; sadness (i.e. mourning) but not especially a violent death

Reversal:

A period of advantage, profit or success but all transient

Page of Swords

Spying; secret service; an indiscreet person

Reversal:

Impostor; cunning; possible sickness; watch out for the unforeseen

Knight of Swords

Active; clever; subtle; martial bravery

Reversal:

Incapacity; impulsiveness; conceit

Queen of Swords

A subtle woman; unswerving; widowhood; not a symbol of mercy or power

Reversal:

Malice; bigotry; deceit; a bad woman with ill will towards the querant

King of Swords

A pure intellect who destroys as soon as he creates; power; command; law; authority

Reversal:

Cruelty; evil intentions; a truth less man

Pentacles

The suit of Pentacles or Disks or Coins represents the element of Earth.

Earth, in the Tarot, is related to things concerning practical or day to day matters. In the Tarot this covers everything from keeping warm and secure, staying fed, healthy and managing our resources. Pentacles also relate to matters of money and employment for, in the modern world, money is the main resource that we use to manage our day to day existence.

The symbol of the Pentacle is clearly representative of a coin. This simple symbolism is fitting, for day to matters should not be tainted with complications of the other elements. Keeping a roof overhead and staying fed should be a simple matter but paradoxically it is one of the things that many people find challenging in life.

A good way to think of the Pentacle is as a solid foundation for the other suits. This is pertinent if the elemental weapons are being used in ritual, particularly so outdoors. A circular Pentacle will rest on almost any uneven surface, so long as it is relatively level. However, standing a top heavy Cup on uneven ground is likely to result in a spillage or worse, whereas placing a flat wide Pentacle on the ground will allow many things, Cups or otherwise, to stand atop it. Of course on a significantly sloping surface anything will topple no matter how solid the foundation, but such a practical lesson is the sort of wisdom that the suit of Pentacles should teach us.

So Pentacles offer us a foundation in life; but we should recognise that management of resources is a continuous juggling act; with the practical development of skills we can provide for our basic needs; and gain security; however the material world can be unpredictable; so prudence is always advisable; wise speculation can lead to profit; and industrious application of skill can lead to much more than basic survival; so that our resources grow; to the point of riches. That is the suit of Pentacles.

Pentacles = Earth = Practicality

Ace of Pentacles

Wealth; gain; material success; opportunity; profit; contentment
Reversal:
The wrong attitude towards wealth; avarice; instability

Two of Pentacles

Harmonious change; balancing resources; material strength
Reversal:
Material weakness; instability

Three of Pentacles

Skilled labour; trade; financial gain; growth
Reversal:
Mediocrity; weakness; pettiness; loss through misdirected effort

Four of Pentacles

Gain; security; sure of ones possessions
Reversal:
Insecurity; opposition; loss

Five of Pentacles

Loss; testing time; material trouble; disorder; the head ruled by the heart

Reversal:

As above but of short duration

Six of Pentacles

Material success; presents; gifts; prudence; nouveau riche; gratification

Reversal:

Tendency to jealousy; threads of prosperity; bribery

Seven of Pentacles

Business; speculation; money; barter; investment; profit; prudence

Reversal:

Impatient; apprehension

Eight of Pentacles

Employment; craftsmanship; skill; competence; making money

Reversal:

Voided ambition; vanity; the skill of the ingenious mind turned to cunning and intrigue

Nine of Pentacles

Safety; success; material arrival

Reversal:

Deception; voided project; deceit

Ten of Pentacles

Gain; riches; family matters; achievements

Reversal:

Gains of hazard; robbery; loss

Page of Pentacles

A dark youth; the bringer of messages; news; student; rule management

Reversal:

Waster; deception

Knight of Pentacles

A useful man; useful discoveries; interest; order; untrustworthy; a brave man unemployed

Reversal:

Inertia; idleness; stagnation

Queen of Pentacles

A dark woman; greatness of soul; generosity; security; a devoted wife

Reversal:

Fear; mistrust; indecision; suspicion

King of Pentacles

Business and intellectual aptitude; mathematical success

Reversal:

An old and vicious man; a dangerous man; weakness; vice; corruption

Major Arcana

The Major Arcana is an altogether different entity. It is often referred to as the fifth suit in the Tarot but, as such, it doesn't really match the other four suits.

Each of the minor suits can be associated with a suit from the modern deck of playing cards. Rods are likened to Clubs, although the symbol has changed somewhat in the modern deck. Cups relate to Hearts with the obvious connections to Water and emotion. The Sword is an edged instrument as is a Spade although the connection is a weak one, while the money represented by Pentacles is easily likened to Diamonds. The Major Arcana, however, has no relationship with modern playing cards.

There are twenty two cards in the Major Arcana instead of the fourteen in each of the Minor Arcana suits. The Minor Arcana can be seen as a progression telling a story through each suit, with the final card from each seeming to link to the first card in the next although these links are ambiguous at best. The Major Arcana, although numbered, is much more difficult to follow and works in a completely different, non linear, way. However, before we can consider the Major Arcana we must talk a little about the Cabala.

The Cabala is a magickal system, a model of the universe (in metaphor), a system for living and many other things all at the same time. To understand the Cabala is a life's work and I'm no expert, but I'll give a brief explanation.

The Cabala is described in the form of a diagram, often called the Tree of Life. It consists of ten spheres joined together by twenty two pathways. Each of the spheres, or sephiroth, represents a concept that might be described as an experience, a state of being or many other things. Understanding the nature of the sephiroth is a major part of cabalistic

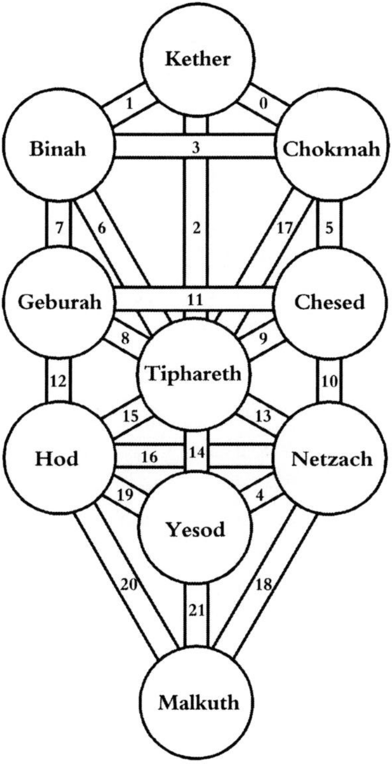

The Tree of Life

study so I'll leave it at that. If you want to know more Google it, and then do some reading, perhaps starting with the same list of luminaries that Nigel and his friends studied when they developed the Tarot definitions in this book.

To study the Tarot we are specifically concerned with the twenty two pathways that connect the sephiroth. Each of these pathways is represented by one of the Major Arcana cards.

Because these twenty two lines form a two dimensional diagram there is more than one way of linking from one location on the tree to another. However, the Cabala is more about the relationships between things than a linier transition between states or concepts as might be seen in the Minor Arcana. This means that there is no single sequence to order the Major Arcana. This then, is a fundamental difference between the Major and the Minor Arcana; there is no set sequence to describe the cards.

Having said that, the Major Arcana are numbered and some students do draw conclusions from the sequence of the numbering. However, the process of maturation that sometimes appears in the Minor Arcana is much less easy to discern with the Major Arcana. Instead the numbers, on the Major Arcana, are used to define their place on the tree.

Just to make life more interesting, various scholars of the mysteries have taken turns at reinterpreting the Cabala and its workings down through the ages and there has been significant disagreement about the numbering, but hey, this isn't an exact science. In fact it's not a science at all, being more of an art; and many people these days think of it as a religion. Of course that depends on what one means by religion, but let's not get into all that religion nonsense right now.

So the pages that follow describe the Tarot definitions defined by Nigel, Geoff and their magickal colleagues in the last millennium. The numbering against the definitions is that which is most commonly used. There is some debate about the cards in positions eight and eleven so Strength and Justice are listed with the alternative numbering. There are other numbers that are disputed but they are much less commonly argued so I have ignored those debates.

Suffice to say, after such a lengthy digression into the Cabala, it is not necessary to take the numbering of any of the cards into account for simple divination. Should you chose to explore the possibility of Tarot for path working or astral travel then these issues will become relevant, but by then you will be a serious student and you will have moved on from the Hidden Master's Pocket Book of Tarot to more significant tomes.

0 The Fool

Spiritual enlightenment; innocence; unworldlyness

Reversal:

A fool in the modern sense

1 The Magician

Skill; wisdom; potential; Mercurial skill; aptitude

Reversal:

Cunning; Trickery; Deception

2 The High Priestess

Intuition; secrets; wisdom; science; mystery; the future as yet unrevealed

Reversal:

Conceit; ignorance; surface knowledge; pretension to spirituality

3 The Empress

Fruitfulness; beauty; success; happiness; generous nature

Reversal:

Waste; idleness; sterility

4 The Emperor

War; victory; conquest; will; ambition

Reversal:

Self control limited; immaturity; impracticability; stubbornness; despotism

5 The Hierophant

Teaching; patience; peace; goodness of heart; kindness

Reversal:

Weakness; over kindness; foolish generosity

6 The Lovers

Impulse; attraction; love; beauty; trials overcome

Reversal:

Failure; indiscretions; foolish designs; self contradiction

7 The Chariot

Events moving in control; single mindedness, focus

Reversal:

Lack of control; distraction

8 (11) Justice

Equilibrium; balance; justice

Reversal:

Injustice; bias; bigotry

9 The Hermit

Retirement from participation in current events; secrecy; caution; prudence

Reversal:

Over prudence; escapism; misanthropy

10 The Wheel of Fortune

Constant change; unexpected luck; chance; the ups-and-downs of life

Reversal:

Ill fortune; failure

11 (8) Strength

Courage; strength; energy; action

Reversal:

Abuse of power; overbearing; cowardice

12 The Hanged Man

Service to others; self sacrifice; intuition; adaptation

Reversal:

Enforced sacrifice; defeat; failure; misplaced loyalty; loss

13 Death

Great change; transformation (often for the better); very rarely physical death

Reversal:

Alteration for the worse; partial change

14 Temperance

Overview; calm consideration; that which tempers, combines and harmonises the psychic and material natures; economy; moderation; management

Reversal:

Disillusion; competing interests; over indulgence

15 The Devil

Temptation; obsession; violence

Reversal:

Evil fatality; weakness; blindness; malicious possession

16 The Tower

Calamity or change; misery; deception; ruin; freedom gained at great cost

Reversal:

The same in a lesser degree; positive change but by great or costly upheaval; tyranny; oppression; imprisonment

17 The Star

Hope; harmony; unexpected help; inspiration, wonder

Reversal:

Hopes not fulfilled; dreaminess; disappointment; provisional living

18 The Moon

Dreams; psychic ability; illusions; deception; hidden enemies

Reversal:

Instability; inconsistency; crisis; lies; delusion

19 The Sun

Triumph; pleasure; glory; gain; riches; joy; contentment; preferred lifestyle

Reversal:

As above but in a lesser degree

20 Judgement

Results; renewal; judgement; sentence; final decision

Reversal:

Weakness; indecision

21 The World

Assured success; the matter in hand; completion; travel; emigration

Reversal:

Fear of change; stagnation; inertia

0 The Fool

Spiritual enlightenment; innocence; unworldlyness

Reversal:

A fool in the modern sense

Support for New Writers

Winged Feet Productions is a small publishing imprint dedicated to bringing you new writers. However, we don't have the resources for promotion or marketing enjoyed by many large organisations; instead we have to rely on word of mouth. If every reader who enjoys Jack's work encourages two friends to buy his books then you can rely on the fact that Jack will be able to continue to get drunk with the Three Hidden Masters, two from Hemel Hempstead and one from Bricket Wood, and perhaps bring you more of their secrets in future volumes.

Find out more by joining our mailing list:

www.productions.wingedfeet.co.uk

Also in the Hidden Masters series

The Hidden Masters and the Unspeakable Evil

Jack Barrow

Clint, Nigel and Wayne, three middle aged master magicians, discover a conspiracy to build casinos in Blackpool, thus making it the Las Vegas of the north, turning the resort into a seedy tacky and depraved town. Heading north at the weekend they need to save the universe by Sunday evening because they have to be back at work on Monday morning.

This is occult fiction with magick and the supernatural, Tarot and astrology, plus grown men in robes performing rituals. All this is wrapped up in Jack Barrow's off-beat wit and quirky perspective on the counter culture of modern occult paganism.

Compared by some to Douglas Adams or Terry Pratchett it is perhaps best described as Harry Potter meets Men Behaving Badly.

ISBN: 978-0-9515329-1-1

Also by Jack Barrow

Satanic Viruses

The fall of the Roman Empire and how to bring it about

Jack Barrow's observations on the changes in the world as we move into the Age of Aquarius. Now in its third edition he uses astrology, Tarot, philosophy, politics and more to examine the nature of the times in which we live.

- Was September 11th a manifestation of the changes that will bring Crowley's New Aeon?
- Has time run out for the major religions of the world?
- Just when did science go loony?
- Was the fall of the Berlin Wall the first major evidence that Armageddon is really underway, and that it won't all be bad?
- Is girl power just one example of the emergence of Crowley's scarlet woman, Spare's primitive woman and Dion Fortune's priestly woman of power?
- Does the existence of international terrorism indicate that the modern scientific paradigm has reached its limits?
- Is the future of humanity dependent or our ability to steer tiny little boats?
- Could YOU change the world with photocopies or spam?

ISBN: 978-0-9515329-3-5

Also from Winged Feet Productions

Kiss of Two Worlds

Alicen Geddes-Ward

Step into Jessamyn Fawn's world ... where the possibility of a secret life in another time is just a thought away. For Jessamyn has unwittingly discovered the key to the Land of Faerie...

A twenty-something librarian living in Suburbia, Jessamyn finds life and conventionality stifling. As a remedy she embarks upon a hidden double life. With the aid of the faeries she reveals more than she ever envisaged about herself and her crumbling marriage to Michael. She and her entangled lover uncover the sparkling answers that a remarkable sexual encounter and the faeries pose. Follow her if you will...

A modern novel inspired by the spiritual marriage of W.B. Yeats and Maud Gonne.

ISBN: 978-0-9515329-2-8

Other material by Alicen Geddes-Ward

Faeriecraft, Hay House, London, 2005.
Co-authored and illustrated by
Neil Geddes-Ward,
(Non-fiction) ISBN 1401905579

Also Music and Meditation CDs

Sleeve notes for Llewellyn and Juliana, *Journey to the Faeries,* New World Music, 2003

Sleeve notes for Llewellyn and Juliana, *Faerie Lore, Journey to the Faerie Ring,* Paradise Music, 2006

The Faerie Cottage: Guided Meditation for Relaxation and Imagination, featuring music by Llewellyn, New World Music, 2004

Journey to the Faerie Ring, Guided Meditations, featuring music by Llewellyn, Paradise Music, 2006

Faerie Workshop, Guided Meditations, featuring music by Llewellyn, Paradise Music, 2006